Gaelic Words in Scots

George McLennan

© George McLennan

First published by New Argyll Publishing 2020

All rights reserved. Without limiting the rights under the copyright reserved above, no part of this publication may be reproduced, stored in, or introduced into a retrieval system, or transmitted in any form or by any means (electronic, mechanical, photocopying, recording, or otherwise) without prior written permission.

For permission requests, please contact
www.newargyllpublishing.com

British Library Cataloguing-in-Publication Data.
A catalogue record for this book is available from the British Library.

ISBN 978-1-907165-42-9

CONTENTS

Preface	5
Introduction	7
Word List	9

Preface

Although this book can stand on its own, it was written as a companion volume to the earlier *Slogans Galore – Gaelic words in English* (New Argyll Publishing 2018). Just as in that volume, I haven't given any pronunciation guidelines. These are adequately dealt with elsewhere and readers may also find *A Gaelic Alphabet* (New Argyll Publishing 2018) helpful. Also, I haven't gone into any great detail regarding features of Gaelic grammar – lenition, spelling etc – since there are many course books and grammars which deal with this. I've mentioned place names, however, on the assumption that some of them will be familiar to many readers, and I've quoted occasional lines of verse or similar where it seemed appropriate. Although dictionaries often have many quotations from local poets and other relatively obscure writers, most will be of limited interest to many readers, so I've restricted mention to a few more well-known figures.

There has been quite a surge of interest in Scots in recent years after decades (centuries?) of discouragement and neglect. Minority languages in Europe are also enjoying a revival of sorts, just as Gaelic has become far more prominent in the last few decades. So this volume highlights both these languages.

George McLennan

GAELIC WORDS IN SCOTS

INTRODUCTION

This book contains a selection of words of Gaelic origin used in Scots. These are to be found in various dictionaries of Scots, as *A Dictionary of the Older Scottish Tongue* and *The Scottish National Dictionary* (SND), both freely available on-line, as well as the *Concise Scots Dictionary*, MacBain's *An Etymological Dictionary of the Gaelic Language* and other works. Some are also to be found in English dictionaries, marked as dialect. Many words in these works are now obsolete, though not, of course, without interest. So I have restricted entries in this present section to words which are attested as being in use in the 20th (and 21st) century, in order to give a reasonably contemporary picture. Many words have more than one meaning, though related, and again I've ignored meanings which are not attested for this more recent period.

A large part of Scotland is not, and never has been Scots-speaking. Roughly put, Scots is the colloquial language of the east and south of the country; the rest of the country is English, and now to a lesser extent, Gaelic speaking. It is worth stressing this point since there was at one time a widespread belief (in England mainly) that Highlanders spoke Scots; in magazines such as Punch they were often the butt of jokes, speaking in sanitized Scots to bemused English visitors. And Sir Walter Scott has Rob Roy, a native Gaelic-speaker, using fluent Scots in his novel of the same name.[1] All very unlikely.

The non-Scots areas are, broadly speaking, Highland Region, Argyll and the Western Isles. Many areas which are now Scots-speaking were Gaelic-speaking in earlier centuries, and there would have been a brief overlap of Gaelic and Scots. In western parts of Aberdeenshire, for instance, there is evidence of this well into the

---

[1] Scott unconvincingly attempted to justify this (Vol 2 Chap 18) by claiming that some Highlanders, when familiar and facetious, used the Lowland Scots dialect.

20th century, but Gaelic has now gone from such places, replaced by Scots and English.

So, many words in dictionaries of Scots are cited from the east and south of the country and aren't part of the language of the north and west. Gaelic-derived words, however, aren't restricted to the north and west but are used in different local areas throughout the country. If they are common enough – e.g. **slàinte** 'health' – they can be heard throughout all Scotland and frequently appear in many English dictionaries.

Most words in dictionaries of Scots have several spellings, many historical (as with most languages) but no longer current. So I've given the most widely acceptable form. Scots suffers in this regard from the fact that there is no agreed national standard, and the pronunciation and spelling of many words differs greatly between, say, Aberdeenshire and Ayrshire. Scots words of Gaelic origin in dictionaries are rarely given in their Gaelic form because there is usually a conflict with Scots or English spelling conventions. So **bealach** is a Gaelic form but can be read and pronounced by a non-Gaelic speaker, whereas **bean-shìth** (or **ban-sìth**) has to appear as banshee.

Some non-Scottish readers may not be too familiar with Scots, so here is a short example from *Johnny Gibb of Gushetneuk* by William Alexander, mentioned below under birse-cup and raith. This classic novel of rural life in the north-east was first published in 1871, went through several later editions/reprintings and is still being published today (2015). Much of the dialogue is written in the Aberdeenshire dialect. Here are the first two lines of the work: 'Heely, heely, Tam, ye glaiket stirk – ye hinna on the hin shelving o' the cairt. Fat hae ye been haiverin at, min?'[2]

---

[2] Stop, stop, Tom, you stupid idiot – you haven't (put) on the hind shelving of the cart. What have you been dawdling at, man?'

WORD LIST

Airie: a shieling, a bothy or hut, often in high pastures used in summer by villagers tending cattle. Gaelic **àirigh**. Common in placenames, as Arinagour, **Àirigh nan Gobhar** 'the Shieling of the Goats', the main settlement and ferry terminal on the isle of Coll. Thomas Pennant, the well-known Welsh naturalist and antiquarian, uses the Gaelic word – which he spells *arrie* – to describe a shieling in Glen Tilt, Perthshire, where he obtained a drink of goat's whey. This account is in his book *A Tour in Scotland 1769*, which describes his first visit to the country; he made a second visit to Scotland in 1772 and again published his experiences. For other words mentioned by Pennant see below under *duchas, lavellan, stoy, struan* and *wag*.

Amitan: a fool. Gaelic **amadan**. The Gaelic word contains the negative prefix a-, as amoral, atheist etc, and a root related to English mind, mental. So, 'mindless'. Being a masculine noun in Gaelic it refers to males; the female equivalent **òinseach** (see under *oanshach* below) refers to women. This distinction continues for the most part in Scots, but at least one dictionary defines *amitan* as 'a fool or mad person, male or female'. This would not look too odd in Scots which doesn't, unlike Gaelic, distinguish nouns by gender.

Auchan: a type of pear. The pear is named after Auchans Castle in Ayrshire where it was first grown, having been imported, probably from France, in the sixteenth century. Gaelic **achaidhean**, 'fields', refers to the open aspect of the now ruined castle. Samuel Johnson and James Boswell visited the castle in 1773 on their tour of Scotland, but don't mention the pear. It was thought to have died out, but in 2003 a variety was found to be growing at Pluscarden Abbey a few miles south of Elgin.

Bat: a flock (of sheep). Gaelic **bad (chaorach)**. The idea of **bad** is a cluster, and usually refers to a copse, a thicket of shrubs, and this is the sense in many place names, as Badachro, **Bad a' Chrò** 'the Copse by the Sheep-fold' near Gairloch, Wester Ross. The word, attested in the south of the country, is thought to have entered Scots from Gaelic-speaking drovers.

Bawcan: a spectre, goblin, ghost. Gaelic **bòcan**. The word is found in Culbokie, **Cùil Bhòcaidh** 'the Nook of the Goblin', a village on the Cromarty Firth side of the Black Isle, and Claybokie, **Cladh Bhòcaidh** 'the Graveyard of the Ghost' a few miles west of Braemar on Deeside.

Bealach: a pass between hills. This is the Gaelic form, but the non-Gaelic form *balloch* is also found. Both are very common in placenames, as Balloch at the south end of Loch Lomond. Another instance, Ballochmyle, **Bealach Maol** 'Bleak Pass' in Ayrshire, was the subject of a couple of poems by Robert Burns (*Farewell to Ballochmyle* and *The Lass of Ballochmyle*). An interesting connection is the phrase *faugh a ballagh* (or *an beallach*), the motto of the Royal Irish Fusiliers (now part of the Royal Irish Regiment). This is a loose version of the Irish **fág an bealach** 'leave a gap, clear the way', a reference to an attack by troops of the regiment during the Napoleonic Wars.

Beeran: a small trout. Gaelic **bioran**, a stick, twig, fairly common in rather obscure placenames, as **Leac nam Bioran** in Kintyre, **Tobar nam Bioran** in Raasay, etc. The Gaelic word is also used of minnows.

Birse-cup: a last cup of tea from the pot, with a dash of whisky or similar added to it. There is some uncertainty about the origin of the phrase; it may be a custom of the village of Birse, near Aboyne in Aberdeenshire, or, more likely, it may be a reference to Mrs Birse, a character in the classic novel of the north-east, *Johnny Gibb of Gushetneuk*, who put some whisky into a friend's cup of tea in order to loosen her tongue. Gaelic **preas** is the origin of the village name (earlier called Bras), which in turn is the origin of the surname. **Preas** 'bush, shrub, thicket' is assumed to have been borrowed from Pictish, since the initial *p* argues against a Gaelic origin, and the location of the village would suit this very well. The Welsh, to which Pictish was related, is *prys*, and an old Welsh/British form is the source of lots of placenames in England (Priston, Prees, Preeze etc) and Wales (Prysol, Prysor etc).

Bladdoch: buttermilk. Gaelic **blàthach**.

Boorach: a mess, shambles. Gaelic **bùrach**. This may be from a later development of the same Gaelic word in the next entry.

Boorag: a sod, turf used as peat. Gaelic **bùrach**, 'a digging'. Booragtoon was an old area of Thurso, so called because the cottages there kept stacks of peat outside, cut from a nearby peat moss. It is apparently still the name of a house there, (in Durness Street), which was at one time the home of Henrietta Munro, a local writer and acquaintance of the Queen Mother, whom she helped to refurbish the nearby castle of Mey.

Boug: belly. Gaelic **bolg, balg**. The general idea is 'bag'. The Gaelic and English words are related, as is *bellows*, for which the Gaelic is also **bolg-sèididh** (blowing bag). **Balg/bolg** is thought to be the origin of the village of Balgy, near Shieldaig, Ross & Cromarty, and also Dunbog in Fife, perhaps referring to some topographical feature. See also *walgan* below.

Bourach: a fetter or rope on a cow's hind legs to prevent it kicking during milking. Gaelic **buarach**. The current Scots spelling is *beerach*, and the use of word is confined to Caithness. The root is **bò**, 'cow', English *bovine* etc.

Brolach: a mess, rubbish. Gaelic **brollach**. The root of the word and the metaphor is from food, as Gaelic **brochan**, 'porridge', and English *broth*. The same idea appears in *farrago*, a mess, from Latin, where it originally meant mash, mixed cattle fodder.

Brot: an apron. Gaelic **brot**. This is a variant of **brat** 'a cloak, mantle, cover'.

Brylocks: cranberries. Gaelic **braoileag**. There is also a form *brawlins*. The Gaelic usually means blaeberry, but also cranberry in some areas. It's a feature of many European languages that the same plant often has different names in different parts of a country.

Buckie, Buckie-faulie: rosehip, briar flower. Gaelic **bòcaidh-fhàileag**. The root of the Gaelic is **bòc** '(to) swell', a reference, presumably, to the swollen buds. The more common Gaelic word for rosehip is **mucan**, from **muc**, 'pig'; in English they are also known as pig noses. See *muckie* below.

Ca: a narrow road or track, a pass. Gaelic **cadha**. Fairly common in placenames, as Camore, **An Cadha Mòr** 'the big track', a mile or so west of Dornoch, Sutherland.

Caib: the iron blade of a spade, peat cutter, cas chrom etc. Gaelic **caibe, ceaba**. This word may possibly be the root of **ceapach**, – now obsolete in Gaelic but still found in Irish – meaning a plot of land for cultivation. As a placename Keppoch it is found in several areas, e.g. Lochaber. The traditional derivation supposes a borrowing from Latin *cippus* 'a block, a boundary stone', which is quite possible – compare the American and Australian use of block to refer to an area of land. Later Irish kept a Latin *p* in borrowings, having earlier replaced it with *c*.

Caibie: the gizzard or craw of a hen. Gaelic **giaban**. Another Scots form *cabin* is nearer the Gaelic.

Cairie: a small breed of sheep found in Caithness. Similar is keerie, a type of sheep found in Orkney, referring to both the famous seaweed-eating North Ronaldsay breed and other less pure breeds. The word is a borrowing from Gaelic **caora** 'sheep'. **Caora** appears in a few placenames, as Meall nan Caorach, a couple of miles south of Amulree, Perthshire. Interesting also are the Caereni, an old British tribe mentioned by Ptolemy (2nd cent. AD, writing in Greek). This is thought to be a reference to sheep (the Old Irish form of the word is *caera*) so they would have been a pastoral people, living on the west coast of Sutherland.

Caochan: a stream; wash, an early unrefined stage of whisky. Gaelic **caochan**. The word is common in Highland stream names. See also *skeechan* below.

Car: left-handed, left-sided. Gaelic **ceàrr** 'wrong, left'. Also *corrie*, especially as corrie-fisted (left-handed). A saying is:

Is fhaid' a làmh cheàrr na a làmh cheart.
'His left hand is longer than his right hand' i.e. he's a thief.

See also *ketach* below.

Clabbydhu: a mussel. Gaelic **clab** 'open mouth' and **dubh** 'black'. Clabbach on the isle of Coll is thought to mean a place with an open aspect.

Claddach: a pebbled river bed or bank. Gaelic **cladach**, a stony beach. Common in placenames, as Cladich, about five miles south-west of Dalmally, Argyll, on a river of the same name.

Cleit; a small round dry-stone building found on St Kilda, used to keep food and peat dry. Gaelic **cleit**, from a Norse word meaning rock, in which sense it is common in placenames, as Clett, a small island near the entrance to Loch Dunvegan, Skye, and Ormaclete in South Uist. Lady Grange was apparently 'housed' for a time in a cleit in the 1730s when her husband removed her from Edinburgh to St Kilda (and other remote locations) to prevent her leaking details of his Jacobite connections. The well-known Skye writer Martin Martin visited the island in 1697 and mentioned cleits and other island matters in his book *A Late Voyage to St Kilda* published a year later. The meaning of the name St Kilda is uncertain and there was certainly no saint of that name. In Gaelic it is **Hiort**, Hirta being the name of the main island, where the inhabitants lived until 1930. A Gaelic phrase is **eadar Hiort agus Peairt** 'between St Kilda and Perth', indicating a vast distance. It's actually about 216 miles, **mar a dh'fhalbhas an ròcas**.

Clip: a young horse, an impertinent child, usually a girl. Gaelic **cliobag** 'a filly'; **-ag** is the feminine diminutive suffix.

Closhach: carcase (of a fowl). Gaelic **closach** 'carcase' (also of animals). Clossach, another Scots form, is closer to the Gaelic.

Clyack: the last sheaf of corn, or other cereal, of a harvest, a widespread custom before the days of combine harvesters. It was decorated with cloth to resemble a girl. Metathesis from Gaelic **caileag** 'a young girl'. There seems, however, to be some confusion between **caileag** and **cailleach** 'old woman'. The latter is the normal word for the above process, appearing in dictionaries, whereas **caileag** is not cited with this meaning in Dwelly and other standard dictionaries. Also, the *y* sound of clyack appears in **cailleach** but not in **caileag**, metathesis notwithstanding. On the other hand there is a reference from Buchan stating that the clyack was either young or old depending on whether the harvest was early or late. Adding to the confusion is the Gaelic word **claidheag** for the last sheaf; MacBain cites it from Badenoch (his local area), says it has been borrowed from Scots, and translates it as 'maiden'.

Coorag[1]: the forefinger, index finger. Gaelic **corrag**. The root of the Gaelic is **còrr** 'pointed', so it's the pointing finger.

Coorag[2]: a woollen hat, a nightcap. Gaelic **currac**. The Gaelic is borrowed from English *curch*, a reduced form of *kerchief*, a covering for the head, usually of cloth. So another instance of Scots borrowing from a Gaelic word which itself is a borrowing from English.

Corcag: a small knife. Gaelic **corcag**, which is the diminutive of **corc**.

Cown: (to) lament, cry. Gaelic **caoin**. From the same Gaelic word comes English *(to) keen*, to lament the dead. Cognate with the Gaelic is English *(to) whine*, an instance of the Gaelic and English initial c/h interchange developed from Indo-European.

Crog: a hand, paw. Gaelic **cròg**.

Croy: a small shellfish. Gaelic **crò-dhearg** 'blood-red'. **Dh** with a slender vowel has a *y* sound in Gaelic; the ending of the word has fallen away in the English. **Crò** is an obsolete word, (but still common in Irish) related to English 'raw' (earlier *hreaw*), showing the *c/h* feature mentioned under **cown** above. **Dearg** is cognate with English *dark*, so it's a deep red.

Cruban[1]: a crab. Gaelic **crùban**. From **crùb** '(to) crouch, bend', cognate with English *creep* and *cripple*; the latter is related to another meaning of **cruban**, a disease in the legs of animals. The general idea is well illustrated by one of the Gaelic words for tortoise, **crùban-coille**. The more usual word **sligeanach** refers to its shell.

Cruban[2]: a wooden frame to fit a horse's back, for carrying hay, peat etc. Gaelic **crùbag**. The reference is presumably to its curved-leg shape, from **crùb** mentioned in the preceding entry.

Crue, also **kro**: a pen or enclosure for sheep or cattle. Gaelic **crò**. Quite common in placenames, as Cromore, **An Crò Mòr** and Crobeg, **An Crò Beag** in the Park district (**Sgìre na Pàirce**) of Lewis, and probably Glen Croe in Argyll which runs south-east from Wade's Rest and be Thankful summit.

Currack: tangle, seaweed. Gaelic **corrag** 'finger', mentioned above under **coorag**[1]. For the metaphor compare the seaweed Dead Man's Fingers, aka Green Sea Fingers, *codium fragile*, and *laminaria digitata*, both of which are common round the coasts of Scotland. See also *slattyvarrie* below.

Cutchack: a small fire. Gaelic **cùilteag** 'a small corner or niche'. The **ch** in cutchack is pronounced as in English, not Scots; this reflects the Gaelic sound of *t* with a slender vowel. The root of **cùilteag** is **cùil** 'a corner, recess', to which the feminine diminutive ending **-ag** has been added. It's a bit surprising that the Scots retains the *t* (and omits the *l*) since strictly speaking the *t* belongs neither to the root nor the suffix of the Gaelic word. But *t* is regularly inserted in this way when suffixes – e.g. plural endings – are added to a word ending in *l*, whether native or borrowed. So **baile** 'town', **bailtean** 'towns', **sgoil** 'school', **sgoiltean** 'schools'.

Cuttag: a dumpy, thickset woman. Gaelic **cutag**. The Gaelic word had been borrowed from the Scots/English word *cutty* with the same meaning, but the diminutive ending **-ag** indicates that Scots *cuttag* has been borrowed from the Gaelic version. Cutty is well-known from the phrase 'cutty sark' (short shirt) used by Burns to describe one of the witches in Tam o Shanter:

And roars out: 'Weel done, Cutty-sark!'
And in an instant all was dark

It was subsequently used as the name of a famous nineteenth century three-masted sailing ship built on the Clyde, as well as a well-known brand of Scotch whisky, the latter probably influenced by the ending of Burns' poem:

Whene'er to drink you are inclined,
Or cutty sarks run in your mind,
Think!

though Burns' words are clearly no endorsement of the product.

Dirken: a fir cone. Gaelic **duircean**, **dorcan**. They were used for smoking fish.

Dirdy-lochrag: a lizard, newt. Gaelic **dearc-luachrach** 'lizard of the rushes, reeds'. **Dearc** should really be **earc**, which it is in Irish, and Dwelly and other lexicographers mention a form **earc-luachrach**. The initial *d* is part of the old form of the definite article which has remained stuck to the noun by wrong division of the words, as also with **deigh** 'ice' (Irish *oighear*) and **dara** or **dàrna** 'second'. Irish too keeps the *d* in *dara*, but this may be because it's an adjective. Whatever the reason, there is no connection with **dà** 'two', in spite of a superficial similarity. In many languages the ordinals *first* and *second* have no etymological connection with the numbers one and two; in Gaelic **ciad** 'first' has the general sense of 'beginning', and **dara** 'second' means *the other* (of two) – a bit like English former and latter. In English *first* means 'foremost' and *second* means 'subsequent, following'. This feature of wrong division occurs also in English with the indefinite article: the above-mentioned *newt* was earlier *an ewt* and a *nickname* was earlier *an ekename*, so the current forms are a mistake. **Luachair** 'rushes' appears in Leuchars, Fife.

Doach: tub, vat. Gaelic **dabhach**. A doach was a cruive, a row of wooden stakes set into and across a river to act as a fish trap. There were three – the meikle, wee and priory doachs – on the river Dee in Kirkcudbrightshire, the last being for the monastery there at one time. **Dabhach** is also an old land measure or capacity, of various sizes, and if this and **dabhach** meaning 'tub' are the same word (as is generally assumed) the connection is thought to be due to the fact that field sizes were defined by the amount of containers of seed, potatoes etc which were required. Not surprisingly the field size reference occurs in several placenames, as Davach of Grange, just east of Keith, Moray, and Fendoch, the site of a Roman camp, about five miles north of Crieff, Perthshire. The forms *davach* and *doch* well illustrate the usual Gaelic option of sounding, or not sounding, an internal *bh*.

Docher: injury, harm. Gaelic **dochair**. The words feature the fairly common Gaelic negative prefix **do-**; so **donas** 'bad luck' from which comes Scots/English *donsie*. This contrasts with **sonas** 'happiness, good fortune'.

Doobrack: a smelt, a young river salmon. Gaelic **dubh-bhreac** can also mean a smelt but is usually a trout. **Dubh** 'black, dark (haired)' is very common of people and as a surname, as (Mac) Duff, Dow etc, as well as a frequent part of placenames, as Duart **Dubhaird**, 'Dark Headland' on Mull. **Breac** 'a trout' is frequent in placenames, as Altnabreac **Allt nam Breac**, 'Trout Burn' in Caithness, about 12 miles south of Dounreay. The basic meaning of the word is speckled, mottled, again a sense in many placenames, as Breachacha **Breac Achadh**, 'Speckled Field' the name of two castles on the island of Coll, Argyll. James Boswell and Samuel Johnson stayed in the newer of the two during their visit to the island in 1773. This meaning of speckled also accounts for the word being used for smallpox (**a' bhreac**) and tartan (**breacan**).

Doorie: a pig; the smallest pig of a litter. Gaelic **durraidh**.

Doss: a bow, knot. Gaelic **dos**. Also *dossan* 'a forelock' from Gaelic **dosan** 'a bunch of hair', a diminutive of **dos**.

Drieshach: red embers of a peat fire. Gaelic **grìosach**. The initial change of letter is unusual, but the SND cites Scots *drodlich* 'a rotting pile' borrowed from Gaelic **grodlach** (from **grod** 'rotten') as a parallel. There is also an occasional initial *d/g* variation within Gaelic itself, as **dreallag** and **greallag**, both 'a swing', which raises the possibility of drieshach reflecting an unattested 'provincial' form ***drìosach**. Drieshach is a surname found in North America, but its meaning is unknown and is unlikely to have any connection with the Scots word.

Drone: the buttocks. Gaelic **dronn** 'rump, back'. **Dronn** is related to **druim** 'back, ridge'; the genitive of **druim** is **droma** and a genitive of **dronn** is **druinne**! In the form *drum* it is quite frequent in placenames, as Tyndrum in Argyll. Dron is a surname and a placename, as Dron **An Dronn**, 'The Ridge', a couple of miles south of Bridge of Earn, Perthshire.

Drowlack: a swing, hammock, a long rope with a seat attached to lower someone over a cliff. Gaelic **drolag** 'a swing', a diminutive of **drola** 'a chain, iron pot-hook'.

Duchas: hereditary right to land. Gaelic **dùthchas**. This was the basis of the clan system in its heyday, until Culloden (1746), and the word is related to **dùthaich** 'country, district'. **Dùthaich MhicAoidh** 'MacKay Country' is a part of Sutherland, occupied historically by the clan of that name. Thomas Pennant (see under *airie* above) mentions duchas, which he describes as landholding 'by a kind of prescribed right'. Pennant correctly connects duchas with **dùthaich** in his footnote to a lengthy speech made to him by the ghost of an old clan chief who describes the clan system to him. Being Welsh Pennant would probably have had an interest in another Celtic language (he quotes several other Gaelic words from time to time) though, surprisingly, he himself knew little Welsh, nor is **dùthchas** related to any Welsh word. It has found a new use today as the name of a whisky from Islay, **Ar Dùthchas** 'Our Heritage'. A proverb says **Is fheàrr dùthchas na gach nì**, 'Heredity is better than everything', though another warns **Is minig a dh'fhàg dùthchas droch ghalar**, 'Heredity has frequently left a bad disease', a variant of *sins of the fathers*.

Durk: a big lump. Gaelic **durc**. Used disparagingly of people. See also *walgan* below.

Eenach: grease in sheep's wool, lanolin. Gaelic **eanach** 'dandruff, down, wool'. It was used in rural districts as a kind of soap and is now an item in luxury soaps.

Eeshan: a toddler, a feeble stunted person. Gaelic **isean** 'a chicken'. The Gaelic is also used of people, usually derogatively. A common expression is **droch isean** 'a bad egg, an unpleasant individual'.

Ess: a waterfall. Gaelic **eas**. Common in placenames, as Bunessan **Bun Easain**, 'the Foot of the Little Waterfall' in the Ross of Mull, and Dalness **Dail an Easa**, 'the Meadow by the Waterfall' half-way down Glen Etive, to the south of Glencoe. Dalness estate was owned at one time by the Fleming family, one of whom, Ian, wrote the James Bond series of novels. Although he lived mainly in London, he is thought to have spent summer holidays at Dalness.

Etnach: of juniper, its berries, wood etc. Gaelic **aiteannach**. **Aiteann** is a juniper tree, the word occurring in Tomatin **Tom Aitinn**, 'Juniper Hillock' a town and distillery about ten miles southeast of Inverness, and Aitnoch **Aitneach**, about eight miles north of Grantown-on-Spey.

Farrach: energy, agitation. Gaelic **farach** 'force, violence'.

Feech: an exclamation of disgust at something unpleasant. Gaelic **f(u)ich** or **fuidh**. Probably onomatopoeic, and found in other European languages, at least as far back as Latin *fi* (second century BC) and English *fie* (thirteenth century) and *faugh* (various spellings, first attested sixteenth century). So it's not clear that the Gaelic has been borrowed from the Scots, nor vice versa. MacBain cites the proverb **cha bhi fuidh ach far am bi fàile**, i.e. the word feech indicates that there's a bad smell about. **Fàile** 'smell' usually has a neutral sense, and would normally require the addition of a word such as **droch** 'bad' to indicate an unpleasant smell. But symmetry is an important feature of proverbs in any language.

Ferintosh: whisky, especially one distilled at Ferintosh on the Black Isle, Ross & Cromarty. Gaelic **Fearann na Tòiseachd**, Land of the Chieftaincy, referring to the creation of a thaneage in the fifteenth century. By the time of the whisky production the estate and distillery were owned by the Forbes clan/family and Ferintosh was the major producer in the north of the country, with an excellent reputation. William Ross, the eighteenth century Gairloch poet, in his poem **Moladh an Uisge-Bheatha** *In Praise of Whisky* calls it

Stuth glan na Tòiseachd, gun truailleadh
'Ferintosh stuff, pure unblended'.

Robert Burns, another connoisseur, laments its demise in Scotch Drink (1785):

'Thee, Ferintosh! O sadly lost!/ Scotland lament frae coast to coast!'

These remarks were prompted by the repeal in 1784 of tax privileges which the British government had granted Ferintosh for nearly a century in return for the Forbes owners' loyalty during the difficult Jacobite times in the Highlands. Financial problems caused by this led to the closure of the distillery shortly later. The name

Ferintosh was used later by other local distilleries, particularly Ben Wyvis, but they too have vanished.

The use of Ferintosh as a general term for whisky was quite common, found, for instance, in Neil Munro's novel *The New Road*, describing events in 1733. Compare the modern use of Cognac, from a specific region in France, as a general term for brandy in many different countries.

Feuach: a poor, sparse crop. Gaelic **fiadhaich** 'wild, uncultivated'. **A' dol fiadhaich** means 'going to seed, shooting' (of plants).

Finnan (haddock): a smoked haddock. Finnan is the local pronunciation of Findon, Kincardineshire, a village known for its smoke-cured fish. The fish was also known as a Findhorn haddock, – so Sir Walter Scott with his customary inaccuracy – by confusion with Findhorn in Moray, another fishing port.

Foorach: buttermilk, whey or cream with added oatmeal, a form of crowdie. Gaelic **fuarag**. The root of the word is **fuar** 'cold' which was how it was usually consumed.

Fowd: poor quality grass left uncut, withered growth. Gaelic **fòd** 'a piece of turf, peat' cut and used as fuel. The word appears in Tilliefoddie 'Hill of the Peats' a small settlement a mile west of Dunecht, Aberdeenshire; and with an alternative form **fàd**, in Faddoch **An Fhàdaich** 'Place of Cut Peats' a couple of miles from the head of Loch Long, Ross & Cromarty.

Freuchan: a toe cap, a reinforced covering for the toe of a shoe or boot. Gaelic **fraochan**. Usually assumed to refer to the toe cap's ability to protect the shoe against the ravages of heather (**fraoch**). The part of the shoe is named after the thing which causes the problem. It's a similar idea to English 'spats' which protect footwear and the lower leg from spatterings of mud etc. A good Scots equivalent to spats is the rustic *nickie tams*, once widely used by farm workers. In North Angus and the Mearns, as I recall, these often took the form of a potato sack of jute or similar fabric, trimmed if necessary and wrapped round the legs from below the bottom of the trousers to below the knee. These were possibly a deluxe version! They were tied in place with a couple of pieces of string and removed at the end of the day, frequently dirty and wet; but the trousers remained relatively clean and dry.[3] **Fraoch** 'heather' appears in several placenames, as Freuchie in Fife and Friockheim in Angus, and Lewis is often called **Eilean Fraoich** 'Heather Island'.[4] It was also the badge of various clans, e.g. MacDonald. See also *sookan* below.

Fuilteach: an indeterminate period of winter, part of January/February or later. Gaelic **faoilteach** had equally vague parameters, but is nowadays restricted to January. This word seems to occur in the small crofting village of Blarmac(h)foldach **Blàr Mach Faoilteach**, about four miles south of Fort William, possibly meaning 'the cold (i.e. wintry) outer field' – perhaps north facing. A saying is:

Smeuran dubha san Fhaoilteach.

'Black brambles in January/February' - of something out of season and highly unlikely.

---

[3] Bothy ballads of the north east mention them, e.g. 'A Pair o Nicky Tams' by G S Morris

[4] Both Lewis and Harris are traditionally described as islands, though each is only a part of the same island.

Gaig: a crack, split, chap (of the hands). Gaelic **gàg**, 'a cleft, crack'. In placenames in means a pass, a gap between hills, as Gaick Pass which goes from Kingussie to Dalnacardach on the A9.

Geenyoch: greedy. Gaelic **gionach**.

Girran: a plouk, pimple, pustule. Gaelic **guirean**. Given the large number of Gaelic names for hills (dozens of these!) it is not surprising to find that this is yet another; so **An Guirean**, a hillock between Fort William and Loch Treig.

Glack: a ravine, hollow, clearing. Gaelic **glac**. Common in placenames, as Glaick, a few miles east of the Kyle of Lochalsh.

Glashan: a young cod, saithe. Gaelic **glaisean**. The root of the word is **glas** 'grey, light green'.

Glaum: (to) snatch, devour, grope. Gaelic **glàm**.

Gnashick: a bearberry, a low plant of the heath family with red berries. Gaelic **cnàimhseag** or **grainnseag**. Although it may seem obvious that the former is the source of the Scots because of the *n*, this borrowing would have had to have taken place when Gaelic initial *cn* kept the n sound; nowadays it would be sounded *cr*. There is also an obsolete Scots form *dognashick*, which again shows the *n*. The Scots words are not attested in literature earlier than the nineteenth century, although they might, of course, have been in common speech long before that. The plant is found on high ground in the Highlands – there is a **Beinn nan Cnàimhseag** about five miles south east of Inchnadamph in Ross and Cromarty. But it is also found on gentler slopes further south judging by the fact that it is a badge of the Colquhouns[5] whose lands lay on the west side of Loch Lomond, and also of the Macintoshes. Nowadays **cnàimhseag** also means a plouk (see *girran* above), acne,

---

[5] The hazel was also their plant badge, according to some sources. There is sometimes apparent disagreement on clan plant badges, possibly due to different septs.

presumably from a resemblance to the small red berries of the plant.

Goich: a disdainful, contemptuous toss of the head. Gaelic **goic**. The Gaelic is borrowed from English *cock* (the head, with the pejorative associations of cocky and cocksure), but the beginning and end of *goich* indicate a borrowing from Gaelic. This English » Gaelic » Scots is an occasional feature; see also *coorag*[2] above, and *pailister, speerack* and *trosk* below.

Golach: a beetle, earwig. Gaelic **gòbhlag**. Scots *hornie golach* is the normal form for an earwig. The Gaelic root is **gobhal** 'fork, bifurcation', cognate with English *gable*, and the reference is to the forked tail of the insect. Glen Goulandie **Gleann Gòbhlandaidh**, a few miles north of Kenmore on Loch Tay, Perthshire, seems to refer to a forked landscape.

Gourlins: earthnuts, pignuts. Gaelic **cutharlan**. There seems to be some confusion, possibly involving metathesis, in the Celtic languages between this word and the word for cucumber, the Gaelic for which is **cularan**, but the related Welsh *cyloryn* and Irish *cúlarán* mean an earthnut. You'd expect to find a native Celtic word for earthnut, but not for cucumber, which even English has borrowed from Latin *cucumis*. But Gaelic **cularan** has the authority of its appearance in the Bible in 1783 (Numbers XI, 5).

Greesh: a stone slab forming the back of a fireplace. Gaelic **grìs** 'fire', which is obsolescent, but modern Irish has *gríos*. Related is *greeshoch*, Gaelic **grìosach** 'burning embers'.

Greeshach: shivering, chilly. Gaelic **grìseach**. The termination of the Scots word suggests that it has been borrowed from Gaelic, although both languages seem to be indebted to English *grise*, 'to shudder', now obsolete but related to modern *grisly*.

Grue: melting ice and snow on rivers and burns. Assumed to be from Gaelic **gruth** 'curds', which it resembles a bit in appearance. There is also, with metathesis, a form *goor*, used of burns choking up with melting ice. The English word *curd*, originally signifying the cheesy part of milk and now extended to other similar substances, is assumed to be borrowed from Gaelic **gruth**, again with metathesis.

Gurr: a squat thickset person. Gaelic **geàrr** 'cut, short, squat'. Common in placenames, as Gairloch **Geàrrloch**, 'Short Loch'.

Hech-how: hemlock. Gaelic **iteodha**. The Scots is a rather unconvincing rendering of the Gaelic word, – the *ch* is Scots (as in loch) whereas the Gaelic *t* has the English *ch* (as in church) – but since both mean 'hemlock' the connection is plausible. The initial and secondary *h* are curious, but Scots sometimes prefixes a word with an unnecessary *h*, as *hit* for *it*, *hoops* for *up* (as an interjection), *hoch* for *och* and so on. Or it's possible that the *h* has resulted from a misunderstanding and misdivision of something like ***lus na h-iteodha**; compare **braoileag**, mentioned above under *brylocks* which also has the form **lus nam braoileag**; **lus** means 'plant'. For other examples of misdivision with the definite article see under *dirdy-lochrag* above. A form like **lus na h-iteodha** requires **iteodha** to be feminine, which it is in the Bible (Hosea X, 4).

Horoyally: a boisterous party, a knees-up. Gaelic **hòro-gheallaidh**. There are different spellings of the Gaelic, which is a meaningless phrase often heard in convivial Gaelic songs.

A fairly modern, twentieth century phrase, though Neil Munro uses it in *The Lost Pibroch* published in 1896.

Ieroe: a great-grandchild. Gaelic **iar-ogha**. **Ogha**, 'grandchild' is the word found in Irish names such as O' Donnell, O' Reilly etc. **Ogha** doesn't really look anything like the Irish O', but the *gh* doesn't belong to the word and is there just to separate the syllables; this happens from time to time in Gaelic. **Iar** is an old word, now obsolete, meaning 'after, beyond'. Burns uses the word in his poem *A Dedication to Gavin Hamilton, Esq.*, and has occasional Gaelic terms elsewhere, as *Ochon(e)* 'alas!' (*To Major Logan*), *duan* 'canto, part of a poem' (*The Vision*) as well as giving the name Luath 'swift', to one of *The Twa Dogs*.

It's unlikely that Burns would have known more than a few words of Gaelic though he probably would have known that it had been spoken in Ayrshire in the previous century. He also wrote several of his poems to tunes with Gaelic titles, so he would at least have known about them and how they sounded. He would also have been constantly reminded of it during his liaison with Mary Campbell (Highland Mary) a native Gaelic speaker from Dunoon, in 1786. A statue of her occupies a prominent position beside the town's castle hill.

Gaelic Words in Scots

Kessock herring: a small herring once caught in the narrows of the Beauly Firth, between North and South Kessock. Gaelic **Ceasag** or similar. St Kessog was a sixth century Irish missionary usually associated with areas further south (Loch Lomond, Perthshire), but the village of Kintessack, also apparently referring to him, is just a few miles along the coast (about eight miles east of Nairn). The surname MacKessock (various spellings) is derived from the saint, though there is sometimes confusion with the name Isaac. More modern references are the Kessock Bridge (1982) and the North Sea Kessog oil field.

Ketach: the left hand. Gaelic **ciotach** 'left-handed'. Coll Ciotach MacDonald, anglicised as Colkitto, was a famous Highland mercenary in the first half of the seventeenth century. **Ciotach** is cognate with Latin *scaevus* (which features an Indo-European moveable *s* – see also *mougre* below), and Scaeva and Scaevola were well-known surnames in ancient Rome, though this did not mean that any bearer of the name was necessarily left-handed. Cognate also is Greek *skaiós*, familiar as the name of the left, i.e. western, gate, the Scaean Gate in Troy, frequently mentioned in Homer's *Iliad*. All this is a fine example of Gaelic's relationship with other Indo-European words over millennia. See also *car* above.

Kirrie Dumplin: the drumstick primula, *primula denticulata*. The Angus town of Kirriemuir is **An Ceathramh Mòr**. The first part means 'a quarter' – referring to land measurement. The flowers, with their rounded shape (like dumplings), were common in Kirrie, as it is known locally. J.M. Barrie, the author of Peter Pan, etc was born here; he referred to the town as Thrums in his pathetic masterpiece *A Window in Thrums*. Thrums were ends of thread and weaving was once the main industry.

Knoud: a gurnard, a sea fish. Gaelic **cnòdan**. The fact that Irish has the same word (*cnúdán*) strongly suggests that Scots is the borrower. The borrowing seems to have taken place when the Gaelic word was pronounced with a *cn* sound at the beginning, to judge from the Scots spelling. This is now pronounced without the *k* sound, and *noud* is also found, but the *kn* combination kept the *k* sound in earlier times. Nowadays initial Gaelic *cn* would usually be pronounced *cr* in both Scotland and Ireland, and there is no sign of this in the Scots.

Lane: a wet, boggy meadow; the water flowing in it. Gaelic **lèan(a)**. The word occurs in Leanaig, a small settlement in the Black Isle, a couple of miles south-east of Conon Bridge, and Lenzie, about five miles north of Glasgow. The *z* in Lenzie was a yogh, pronounced – but no longer! – like a *y*.

Larach: a site, ruins of a building. Gaelic **làrach**, the root of which is **làr** 'ground, floor', cognate with English 'floor'. Fairly common in placenames, as Crianlarich, **A' Chrìon Làraich** 'The Shrunken, Withered Site', about ten miles to the north of Loch Lomond.

The differences between the Gaelic and English versions of the name illustrate a couple of fairly common points: the Gaelic genitive **làraich** is not very grammatical but may represent local pronunciation, and English versions of Gaelic names are seldom 100% accurate; and the town was, and often still is, called Crianlarach. Larachbeg is another example of anglicised liberties; since **làrach** is feminine you might expect Larachveg **A' Làrach Bheag** 'the small site' but again the English version of Gaelic names often ignore such nuances. This village, about four miles north of Lochaline in Morvern became the new home for most of the St Kildans, where the men were employed by the Forestry Commission. Many of them had never seen a tree before, St Kilda being treeless.

The poet Hugh McDiarmid (C.M.Grieve) uses the word in *Sangschaw: 'Earth's littered wi' larochs o' Empires'*.

Lavellan: a water-shrew. Gaelic **lamhalan** (various spellings). Thomas Pennant (see under *airie* above) asked about this animal while staying in Ousdale (which he calls Ausdale), a small village about five miles south-west of Berriedale, Caithness. He suspects that it is a water shrew-mouse, the same animal as the water mole in nearby Sutherland. Rob Donn, the eighteenth century Sutherland poet mentions the creature in his humorous poem **Briogais MhicRuaraidh**, the said MacRory having lost his trousers. The poet is concerned about the trouserless MacRory being molested by a **lamhalan** – there was a legend of a larger noxious version of this animal.

Leck: a stone slab, flagstone, tidal rock ledge. Gaelic **leac**. The word occurs in crom<u>lech,</u> a word of Welsh origin, meaning a stone circle, or, formerly, a dolmen; an anglicized plural – Gaelic plurals don't end with an added s – occurs in Cromlix, an estate a few miles north of Dunblane, Perthshire. **Leac** itself is found in a few placenames, the best known being the ski resort of Lecht near Tomintoul, Moray.

Loorach: a worn, tattered coat; its wearer, a dishevelled person. Gaelic **lùireach**. The Gaelic was borrowed from Latin *lorica*, a leather cuirass made from thongs and bits of metal, standard issue to Roman legions.

Lorne shoe: a strong type of shoe, still available. Named in honour of the Marquis of Lorne, Gaelic **Latharna**. This is the title of the eldest son of the Duke of Argyll; in 1871 the then marquis, after whom the shoe was named, married Queen Victoria's daughter Louise. Lorne is a part of the county of Argyll, with Oban as its main town.

Lunkart: a temporary shelter or bothy. This word seems to be a conflation of two Gaelic words **longphort** and **lùchairt**, since it more resembles the latter but retains the *n* of the former.

The original meaning of **longphort** was harbour, haven, from **long** 'a ship' and **port** 'harbour' (both words borrowed from Latin). From the meaning *haven* both the sense and the word developed to *shelter, camp*, then *dwelling, palace*. So **lùchairt** is a development from earlier **longphort**, with denasalisation (dropping the *n*) and a compensatory lengthening (*ù*). This latter feature usually represents a development of the word from its earlier old or middle Gaelic form, so it's surprising to see **longphort** in Dwelly. And although more modern dictionaries don't include the word, it appears in modern Irish (*longfort* 'a stronghold'). Luncarty in Perthshire is **Longartaidh** 'Camp', with a reference to the temporary camp of invading Danish ships (**long**) in 980.

Machreach: a bother, squabble. Gaelic **mo chreach!** The Gaelic interjection means 'oh dear, alas!' It is also commonly extended to **mo chreach-sa thàinig!** 'good grief!'. **Creach** means 'a raid, plunder, booty'.

Maig: a paw, large hand. Gaelic **màg**. The Gaelic is related to English *manual*, *manufacture* etc; early Celtic seems to have added a stem suffix *k-*, giving a form *mank-*. In Gaelic the *n* then disappears, with a compensatory vowel lengthening. See under *lunkart* above. This has happened with other Gaelic words, as **òg**, cognate with English *young*.

Mant: to stutter, stammer. Gaelic **manntach** 'stuttering'. Related is English *mandible*, a jaw(bone). In his novel *The Shoes of Fortune* Neil Munro (see under *Ferintosh* and *Horoyally* above) describes a minister as 'him wi' the mant i' the Tron Kirk' - an unfortunate affliction for a preacher, if not quite in the Spooner class.

Meenie: an awl. Gaelic **minidh**. A sharp tool used by cobblers for piercing leather etc. A saying is:

Cho geur ri minidh 'Ic Eachainn.
'As sharp as MacEachainn's awl'.

Melg: milt, the roe of male fish. Gaelic **mealg**. A connection with English *melt* is likely.

Micken: spignel, baldmoney, a small plant with white flowers. Gaelic **muilceann**. Aromatic and edible, both flower and root. Mickenbaulks (Spignel Ridge) was once part of the farm of Over Auchenleish in Glen Isla on the Angus/Perthshire border.

Mink: a snare, halter, tether. Gaelic **muince**. Related words are **muineal** 'neck', **muinghiall** 'headstall of a bridle' and **muing** 'mane (of a horse)'.

Mougre: to be sullen, gloom-laden. Gaelic **mùig** 'gloom'.

Mowrie: shingle, a beach of sandy shingle. Gaelic **morghan** 'shingle, pebble beach' and **mormhach** 'land liable to flooding by the sea' are assumed to account for the Scots borrowing. The basis is **muir** 'sea', common in placenames, as Morvern, Moray. **Mormhach** occurs in **A' Mhormhaich** 'Lovat', the area round Beauly on the Beauly firth and river. Lord Lovat is the title of the chief of Clan Fraser.

Muckie: a rose hip. Gaelic **mucag**, from **muc** 'pig'. As indicated under *buckie* above the fruit is also known as pig noses, from some apparent resemblance. *Muckie* shows the Scots diminutive suffix; another form *muckack* reflects the Gaelic.

Mullach: my dear. Gaelic **muileach** 'dear, beloved'. A rather rare word in both languages, generally used by women to each other. Compare the now obsolete English *mulling* and *mully* used as terms of endearment (*darling* etc), and of a child to its mother. Although Gaelic borrowing from English goes back a long way – fifteenth century and possibly earlier – this doesn't seem too likely here, given the word's rarity (there's also a noun **muileag** 'dear lady') and its quoted location of Caithness, which would suggest Norse rather than English origin.

Muskan: a razor-fish. Gaelic **mùsgan**, **muirsgian**, the latter showing more clearly the meaning of sea (**muir**) knife (**sgian**). **Tràigh nam Mùsgan** 'Razor-fish Beach' is on Asknish Bay, about fifteen miles south of Oban, Argyll.

Oanshach: a foolish person. Gaelic **òinseach**, regarded as the feminine equivalent of **amadan** (amitan) above. The feminine suffix **-seach** is found in a few words, the masculine of which is a different word, as **amadan/òinseach**; so **boc/maoiseach** (buck/doe) and **lon-dubh/cèirseach** (blackbird/hen blackbird[6]). Unlike Gaelic, *oanshach* in Scots is not restricted to females. The former settlement of Strontoiller, about four miles east of Oban, was full of such women, according to the saying **Is iomadh òinseach tha 'n Sròn Toilleir**; nowadays it's more known for its stone circle dating from the second millennium B.C. The Gaelic saying may in fact be a vague reference to an ancient folk memory of the stone circle representing women who had been petrified because of some misdemeanour or folly. This idea was a later 'explanation' of some stone circles of neolithic Britain, as the Merry Maidens circle and the Nine Maidens of Boskednan circle, both in Cornwall. In this country the famous standing stones at Callanish, Lewis, were in earlier centuries referred to as **Na Fir Bhrèige** 'The Liars', one theory being that they were men who had been petrified for denying Christianity.

---

[6] This is really more Irish than Gaelic; in Gaelic the meaning is thrush or woodlark.

Pailister: a game of skittles. Gaelic **peilistear**. Often translated as 'quoit(s)', which, however, are small hoops of iron (or nowadays plastic etc) thrown to encircle a peg in the ground. References to pailister always indicate pebbles, which are thrown to hit or land as near as possible to the peg. Not unlike petanque or boules. **Peilistear** may be an extension of earlier **peilear** 'a ball', but the initial *p* indicates that it isn't a native Gaelic word. So this is another example of Gaelic borrowing a word (from French in this instance), which is then borrowed by Scots from Gaelic; see also under *goich* above.

Pickie: a young saithe or coalfish. Gaelic **piocach**, which is also used to describe a small person, according to Dwelly. As the *p* indicates, the Gaelic is borrowed, presumably from English. Probably related to English *pick* with its connotations of smallness (pick at one's food) or the Romance language root *pic* (*piccaninny*, *piccolo* etc), or perhaps the word *pigmy*, widely used in English since the seventeenth century to indicate small versions of birds, animals, whales etc. The simple combination -*gm*- in *pigmy* is not found in modern Gaelic; the *m* would be lenited and then frequently not sounded.

Pran: to crush, bruise, pound. Gaelic **prann**. Related is the more specialized *pron* 'husks and other remains of oats after milling', from Gaelic **pronn**, an alternative spelling of **prann**.

Both words would have the same pronunciation in many areas, e.g. Lewis. *Pronack* **pronnag** is 'a crumb, any messy waste'.

Quigrich: the pastoral staff of St Fillan. Gaelic **coigreach** 'foreigner, stranger'. St Fillan was an eighth century Irish saint who lived and worked most of his life in Scotland. The curved head of the staff or crozier can be seen in the National Museum of Antiquities, Edinburgh. There is really no convincing explanation of the staff's name; it was said, for instance, to have magical powers to identify stolen property now among foreigners, or it was for centuries in possession of the clan Dewar, whose name means *pilgrim, foreigner, exile*.

Raith: a quarter of a year. Gaelic **ràithe**. From the same root as **ruith** 'run', i.e. a course of the year. The root appears in **samhradh** 'summer' and **geamhradh** 'winter'. *Raith* occurs several times in William Alexander's novel *Johnny Gibb of Gushetneuk* quoted in the introduction above. A saying is:

Ciad Luain na ràithe,
seall nach fhàg an rath do thaigh.
'On the first Monday of a quarter
see that good fortune doesn't leave your house'.

It was believed that people with the Evil Eye were greatly empowered on such a day. Gaelic, like other languages, had a number of days which were propitious, or unpropitious, for doing various things.

Rannoch: fern, bracken. Gaelic **raineach**. Related, with metathesis, to English *fern*, showing each language's typical treatment of initial *p* in Indo-European; Gaelic loses the *p* whereas English changes it to *f*. So **athair**/father, **làr**/floor, **iasg**/fish and so on. The word is common in placenames, as Rannoch, Perthshire.

Rauchan: a plaid worn over the shoulders. Gaelic **rachdan**.

Reesk: coarse grass, reeds etc; rough ground on which they grow. Gaelic **riasg**. Related is English *rush* (earlier *risce*). **Riasg Buidhe** is a former settlement on Colonsay, abandoned in 1918. Most of the houses still remain, though now roofless.

Riach: drab, greyish white, streaked. Gaelic **riabhach**. This is the origin of the surname Riach or Reoch, presumably originally referring to hair colour. **An Riabhach** was one of the many euphemisms for the devil, Satan. Fairly common in placenames, as Clackriach, **Clach Riabhach** 'Brindled Stone', about three miles south east of New Deer, Aberdeenshire, and Dalreavoch **An Dail Riabhach** 'The Brindled Dale' about ten miles west of Brora,

Sutherland. The latter shows the less usual (but perfectly correct) pronunciation of **riabhach** with the **bh** sounded.

Ropach: grotty, dishevelled. Gaelic **robach**.

Rothick: a small crab. Gaelic **rudhag** 'little red thing', based on the root **ruadh** 'red' with the feminine diminutive suffix **-ag**. Other Scots forms *ruthag* and *roddack* are nearer the Gaelic.

Roy: rot in conifers. Gaelic **ruaidhe** 'redness' from the same root as the previous entry. A reddish disease of the trunk, particularly in larches. **Ruaidhe** also refers to other red or inflamed features as erysipelas, shingles, herpes and rash.

Ruskie: a straw basket, straw sunhat, straw beehive (a skep). Gaelic **rùsgan**. The basis of the word is **rùsg** 'bark, husk, outer cover'. The now rare English *ruskin* 'a tub or basket made of bark to hold butter' is borrowed from Irish. French and obsolete Scots *ruche* 'a beehive' is thought to be derived from an early Celtic word meaning 'frill, pleat' from the similarity to lengths of straw, reed etc, or else from a late Latin word for *reed, rush*, and probably connected with **rùsg**.

Scag: to become weather-beaten, wrinkled (of the face). Gaelic **sgag** '(to) crack, split'.

Scallag: a farm labourer. Gaelic **sgalag** 'a servant, skivvy'. The Gaelic is borrowed from a Norse root seen also in English mar*shal*, originally meaning mare (horse) servant, i.e. groom, farrier etc. There is a Beinn nan Sgal(l)ag with associated loch and airidh just east of Tolsta Chaolais in Lewis. Neil Munro (see under *ferintosh* above) calls landless folk scalags in *The New Road*. **Sgalag** is unusual, if not unique, in being a feminine noun but referring mostly to males.

Scarnach: a crowd of people, or a large heap of stones. Gaelic **sgàirneach**. The root of the word seems to be **gàir**, 'noise, din', referring to the sound of a crowd of people, or of stones falling down a hillside. The word earlier meant scree, loose stones on a hillside. If so, **sgàirneach** is another instance of a 'movable' Indo-European *s* (see under *ketach* above), though you might have expected the *s* to be in **gàir** also.

Scattan: herring. Gaelic **sgadan**. The word is related to English fish names scad, shad and skate. Garscadden, **Gart Sgadain** 'Herring Yard', now part of Glasgow, was presumably once the site of a herring market. A Gaelic saying about the relative size and nutritional value of various sea creatures begins:

> **Seachd sgadain, sàth bradain**
> **Seachd bradain, sàth ròin...**
> 'Seven herring will satisfy a salmon,
> seven salmon will satisfy a seal...'

Scob: a pliable twig of hazel or willow to make baskets, roof thatch pegs, splints etc. Gaelic **sgolb** 'a splinter, wattle'. From the Gaelic/Irish is English scallop 'a thatch pin'. Rescobie Loch near Forfar, Angus is thought to be **Ros Sgolban** 'Woodland of Splinters, Thorns', which were once nearby.

Scoskie: starfish. A rather garbled version of Gaelic **crosgan**. The root is **crois** 'cross', from its shape.

Scraw: a turf, sod, divot used for roofing. Gaelic **sgrath**.

Scriddan: a mountain burn, loose stones and gravel on a hillside, scree. Gaelic **sgrìodan**.

This is presumably the meaning of Loch Scridain in the southwest of Mull, a relatively recent name. In Blaeu's atlas of 1654 (largely based on the maps of Timothy Pont – **a bha thall agus a chunnaic** – compiled towards the end of the previous century) it is called Loch Leffan. This looks like a reference to the area at the head of the loch, **leth fhonn** 'half land'; it's a swampy terrain with a ford running through it, **An Leth-Onn** on the current O.S map. Or it could be another *lephin* (a land measurement placename) now vanished from here, but still found in the north of the island and elsewhere. The nearby Loch na Keal is also a new(ish) name; Blaeu calls it Loch Scaffort.

Scroban: the crop or gullet of a bird or human, craw. Gaelic **sgròban**. The Gaelic looks like another instance of moveable *s* (see under ketach above) based on English *crop*, with the Gaelic masculine diminutive **-an**.

Shannack: a bonfire, especially at Hallowe'en. Gaelic **samhnag**. The basis of the word is **samhain**, now November; **Oidhche Shamhna** is Hallowe'en. The first part of **Samhain** is cognate with English summer, while the second part is the now obsolete **fuin** 'end' – a lenited *f* loses its *f* sound, hence the modern form **samhain** (formerly **samhuin(n)**). A saying is:

Oidhche Shamhna theirear gamhna ris na laoigh.

'At Hallowe'en the calves are now called stirks'.

Gaelic, like many other languages, is full of different words for sheep, cattle, fish etc at various stages of their development. See also *sownack* below.

Sharg: a puny, stunted person. Gaelic **searg**. Also *shargar*, signifying the runt of a litter, Gaelic **seargair**. The general idea is decay, witheredness.

Sharrow: bitter, tart. Gaelic **searbh**. Distantly related to English *sour, sorrel*. A good instance of the common Gaelic pronunciation of final **-bh** as /u/ (as in *root*). Manx, which is closely related to Gaelic but is written in an English-based phonetic script, spells the word *sharroo*.

Shimee: a straw rope. Gaelic **sìoman**. This, like *simmen, simmonds* etc. with the same meaning, is borrowed from Norse, but the form of *shimee* with the Gaelic-influenced initial *sh* sound strongly suggests that it has been taken directly from Gaelic. Simmen, simmonds etc have come straight from Norse and are found in the Northern Isles (and elsewhere). There is an English dialect form *sime*, also from Norse. Usually a rope of two twisted strands, in contrast to the *sookan* (see below). A saying is:

Cho mear ri ceann sìomain rè latha gaothach.

'As frisky as the end of a straw rope on a windy day'.

Sithean: a hillock, tumulus, especially one in which fairies were thought to live. Gaelic **sìthean**. The basis is **sìth** 'a fairy', found also in *ban<u>shee</u>* 'a female fairy'. Common in placenames, as Glen Shee (Angus/Perthshire), Strontian **Sròn an t-Sìthein** 'Promontory of the Fairy Hill' in Sunart, and Schiehallion **Sìth Chailleann** 'the Fairy Hill of the Caledonians, in Perthshire. Fairies were widely believed in, and could cause trouble but also bestow gifts. A saying is: **Bhean a' bhan-shìthiche ris** 'The fairy woman touched him', thus giving him possession of the evil eye. On the other hand a female fairy gave one of the earlier MacCrimmons a silver chanter which enabled him to outperform any other piper. This continued with many generations of the family, and led to the founding of their famous piping college at Boreraig in Skye, and their role as hereditary pipers to McLeod of Dunvegan. Their famous **Bratach Shìth** 'Fairy Flag', supposed to have been a gift from a fairy, can still be seen at Dunvegan castle.

Siven: a wild raspberry. Gaelic **suibhean**, a masculine form of the more usual **suibheag**. The root is **sùbh** 'berry'. This is thought to be part of the meaning of (Kin)Loch Hourn in Knoydart, particularly in view of **Coire Shùbh** nearby. English cognates from forms of the same Indo-European root are *sup, soup* and *suck*.

Skathie: a wooden fence used as a windbreak over an opening such as a doorway. Gaelic **sgàth** 'a hurdle, wattled door'. *Skathie* has the typical Scots diminutive suffix *-ie*.

Skeechan: an inferior kind of liquor produced as part of the brewing process, often improved by adding treacle to make a sort of beer. Gaelic **caochan** (see above), with Scots variant *keechan*, – though this refers to distilling, not brewing – to which an initial *s* has been added. This movable *s* (see under *ketach* above), often referred to as prothetic *s*, is not uncommon in Scots also, as spink/pink etc.

Skelb: a splinter or fragment of wood, stone, metal etc, especially one penetrating the skin. Gaelic **sgealb**. Another, and more usual, Scots form is *skelf*. English *spelk* 'a splinter' doesn't indicate metathesis, since the Germanic cognates all begin *sp-*. Probably related is English *shale* 'rock splinters', showing typical Germanic *sh/sk* interchange, as *shirt/skirt* etc. This also reinforces the view that *shelf* is related to *skelf*, the idea being that it, shelf, is a flat thin slab.

Gaelic Words in Scots

Skippie: the game of tig. Gaelic **sgiobag**, noted by Fr Allan McDonald[7] as 'a children's game, tig'. Another Scots form *skippack* is closer to the Gaelic. The general idea is 'snatch at, touch rapidly'.

Slattyvarrie: oakweed, *laminaria digitata*, an edible seaweed. Gaelic **slat-mhara** 'rod of the sea'. **Slat** is cognate with English *lath* and **mara** is cognate with English *marine* etc. Common round the west coast and islands. See also *currack* above.

Slock: a hill pass, hollow between hills, an inlet between sea rocks. Gaelic **sloc**. A feature of placenames, as Slockavullin, **Sloc a' Mhuilinn** 'the Hollow of the Mill', a mile or so south-west of Kilmartin, Argyll. Another Scots form *slug* appears in the Slug Road, the A957 between Stonehaven and the A93, a few miles east of Banchory. The pass in question lies between Craigbeg and Cairn-mon-earn hills, both over 1000ft, about half way along the road.

Smiach: a word, sound, power of speech. Gaelic **smiach**. Scots follows Gaelic in using the word only in negative phrases – not a smiach from him/**chan eil smiach aige**.

Smurach: dust, dross, crumbled peat. Gaelic **smùrach**. Lochan Smurach, about ten miles north of Ullapool, just east of the A835 at Drumrunie Lodge, presumably has, or had, a bed and surround of dusty peat fragments.

Sookan: a straw rope. Gaelic **sùgan**, a twisted rope of one strand, contrasting with the double-stranded *shimee* (see above). *Sookans* were often used, in Orkney at least, to protect footwear and legs; the rope was wound under the instep, over the top of the shoe and round the ankles and lower leg. This helped to keep feet dry when walking through snow, puddles etc. See also *freuchan* above.

---

[7] Gaelic Words and Expressions from South Uist and Eriskay

Sornie: the flue of a kiln, its fireplace. Gaelic **sòrn**. *Sornie* has the typical Scots diminutive suffix *-ie*, the equivalent of Gaelic **sòrnag**. The Ayrshire village of Sorn 'kiln' is about five miles east of Mauchline. There is a local tradition, however, that the village, named after nearby Sorn castle, has a reference to a promontory or high ground, which describes the situation of the castle. This looks like a confusion (metathesis?) between **sòrn** and **sròn**, promontory being one of the meanings of the latter, though both words have – or had – the meaning *nose, snout*; today **sròn** is the form used.

Sownack: a Hallowe'en bonfire, a flaming fir torch used on such occasions. Gaelic **samhnag**. See under *shannack* above.

Spag: a paw or hand, a foot. Gaelic **spàg**, also 'a claw'. There is also a form **spòg**, which Scots has borrowed as *spyog*, of similar meaning. There are subtle differences within both languages however; splay-footed is normally **spàgach**, but the hand of a clock is **spòg**. In Scots, *spyog*, but not *spag*, can be used to describe a dead short branch of a tree. The *p* in the Gaelic words means that the word has been borrowed, possibly from Latin via Welsh; modern Welsh *bach*, 'a hook, crozier, bishop/shepherd's crook' may well be connected with Latin *baculum* 'staff, crozier'. The prothetic *s* of **spàg** (see under *skeechan* above) is not a problem, but the short *a* of *baculum* is, since the vowel of **spàg** is obviously long. Sir Walter Scott in his tale of *The Two Drovers* (1827) uses *spyog* (in the form *spiog*) to describe legs wearing tartan hose.

Spatchell: spruce, natty, smartly dressed. Gaelic **spaideil**. As the *p* indicates, the word is borrowed, ultimately from Latin. There seems to be some sort of distant connection with Italian *spaziare* 'to promenade' particularly with reference to the evening stroll performed by Italians wearing their finest clothes or latest acquisitions in order to make a fashion statement. The idea is 'to swagger'. Borrowed also is English *expatiate* 'to walk about'.

Speerack: an alert, energetic person. Gaelic **speireag** 'a sparrow-hawk', borrowed from English. This is a reference to the qualities of the bird, as instanced by phrases like as watchful as a hawk and as swift as a hawk. In Gaelic the word also means a tall slender girl, but in Scots *speerack* can be any lively person, despite the *-ack* suffix reflecting the Gaelic feminine suffix **-ag**. For this feature see also *amitan* and *oanshach* above. The sparrow-hawk gives its name to a couple of hills – **Creag nam Speireag** – about five miles east of Ullapool and again in the Braes of Balquhidder, just north of Loch Voil. *Speerack* is another instance of Scots borrowing a Gaelic word which was itself borrowed from English. See under *goich* above.

Stoy: a buoy or float placed to indicate the position of sunken lobster pots, fishing lines etc. Gaelic **stuthaidh**. Thomas Pennant (see under *airie* above) uses the word, which he calls *stuoy* and first heard about in Campbeltown, to describe lines eighty fathoms long placed at each end of the fishing lines, and marked with buoys.

Struan: a round cake once made at Michaelmas, 29th September, using cereals and other fruits from local farms. Gaelic **strùthan**. A symbolic ritual, with various incantations, to celebrate the completion of the harvest, even if not everything had been gathered in due to a late harvest. Found latterly in Roman Catholic areas, e.g. South Uist, Barra. Thomas Pennant (see under *airie* above) mentions it – as Struan-Micheil – during his account of a visit to Canna.

Tarbe(r)t: an isthmus. Gaelic **tairbeart**. The idea is 'bringing over', historically appropriate in the case of Tarbert Loch Fyne, Argyll, where the Viking Magnus 'Barefoot' had his ship carried across the isthmus there to allow him to claim Kintyre as an island. Tarbet is another well-known isthmus, between Loch Lomond and Loch Long, but there are many less well-known others, e.g. in the islands of Gigha and Jura.

Tarleather: a long thin piece of animal hide, cut from the belly for use as a strap etc. Gaelic **tàrr** and **leathar**. **Tàrr** 'belly' is cognate with English *tharm*, Scots *thairm* (Burns *Address to a Haggis* – 'painch, tripe or thairm') and **leathar**, or its earlier Celtic form, was borrowed by the Germanic language family, hence English *leather*.

Torr: an embellished projection, an ornamental protruding addition, an ornamental piece of wood. Gaelic **tòrr**, 'hill, heap'. The Scots meaning relates to the Gaelic diminutive **torran** 'a knob'.

Trosk: a dim-witted, rambling person. Gaelic **trosg**. The main meaning of **trosg** is cod-fish, but it also has the secondary sense of a dull, lumpish person. The word is cognate with English *torsk, tusk*, a fish of the cod family, which, like Gaelic **trosg**, were borrowed from Old Norse. So this is another example of a Scots word borrowed from a Gaelic word which was itself borrowed. The word appears in <u>Tarsk</u>avaig 'Cod Bay' in the Sleat peninsula of Skye.

Truaghan: a poor wretch, a pitiful fellow. Gaelic **truaghan**, used of males. The feminine suffix **-ag** gives **truaghag** 'a wretched female'. English *truant*, a borrowing from Old French, is thought to be cognate, a Celtic source being the origin.

Trusdar: a villain, 'bad egg', nasty piece of work. Gaelic **trustar**. Scots also has *trushlach* and *trooshter*, the latter used of annoying children, brats.

Tuchin: hoarseness, a rough cough, hawking. Gaelic **tùchan**. Probably onomatopoeic.

Tulloch: a hillock. Gaelic **tulach**. Frequent in place names, where it usually takes the forms Tilly-, Tulli-, or Tully- in English. So Tillicoultry etc.

Tummock: a small heap of earth or grass, a knoll. Gaelic **tom**, common in place names, as Tomintoul **Tom an t-Sabhail** 'the Hillock with the Barn'. The suffix -*ock* is common in Scots, sometimes confused with or influenced by the Gaelic diminutive suffix -*ag*, but **toman** rather than **tomag** is the usual Gaelic form.

Tusk: to empty out, pour out. Gaelic **taosg**.

Urlar: the ground or theme in pibroch which begins the tune and provides the basis for the variations which follow. Gaelic **ùrlar**. The root of the word is **làr** 'floor', and the Gaelic and English words are related; English words beginning with f often have Gaelic cognates without the f, as **athair**/father, **leathann**/flat etc.

Wag: a ruined iron-age structure, partly below ground level, to house people and/or livestock, or to store produce. Gaelic **uamhag** 'a little cave'.

Wags are found in Caithness; there is a ruined and long-abandoned settlement at Wagmore, about nine miles west of Dunbeath. They are often found beside brochs, the round stone iron-age towers peculiar to Scotland. Thomas Pennant (see under *airie* above) adds an appendix, written by the Rev Alexander Pope, minister of Reay, to his 1769 tour account. The minister describes them and their locations in some detail, and adds that they are locally called *uags*. The basis of the word is **ua(i)mh** 'cave', often appearing in place names as Weem – so Wemyss in Fife – but the Gaelic form appears in **Loch nan Uamh** near Arisaig, from where Prince Charles Edward Stuart finally left Scotland in 1746, and **An Uamh Bhinn** 'the melodious cave', known in English as Fingal's cave, on Staffa in the Inner Hebrides. The diminutive **uamhag** is less common, but an instance is **Loch na h-Uamhaig**, a couple of miles north of Diabeg in Torridon.

Walgan: a bag, sack, a 'lump', i.e. a big dull leaden person. Gaelic **balgan** 'a little bag', cognate with English belly, bellows and bulge. This aspect of *walgan*, with its suggestion of a fair size, is rather at variance with **balgan**, the diminutive form of **balg**. It's also strange to find an initial Gaelic *b* represented by *w*; a lenited *b* (i.e. *bh*) sometimes has the sound of an English *w*, but only in the middle of a word. You can see this in the common surname **Mac a' Ghobhainn**, anglicized as MacGowan, Gowan, Gow and other forms; it's also frequently translated as Smith (Scotland's most common surname), since **gobha** is a (black)smith. It's true that Gaelic sometimes uses *b* in place of English *w* (which isn't in the Gaelic alphabet) in its version of modern English words, as **barantas**/warranty, **buaic**/wick etc. But *walgan* from **balgan** is the other way round. See also *boug* and *durk* above.

Finally, it's worth mentioning that the traffic isn't always one-way. Modern Gaelic has sometimes borrowed from the Scots version of a word (possibly sometimes influenced by Old French or Old Norse) rather than the modern English form. Some examples in common use today are:

bruis (brush), **cuaraidh** (quarry), **cùirt** (a court), **cunnt** (count), **crùn** (crown), **dusan** (dozen), **flùr** (flower), **làraidh** (lorry), **leadaidh** (lady), **poileas** (police), **punnd** (a pound), **pùdar** (powder), **reusan** (reason), **sàsar** (saucer), **saighdear** (soldier), **sguad** (squad), **tràlair** (trawler), **unnsa** (ounce). The English words cited have a different vowel sound in Scots and this is then reproduced in the Gaelic version.

www.ingramcontent.com/pod-product-compliance
Lightning Source LLC
Chambersburg PA
CBHW071757080526
44588CB00013B/2282